WHAT YOUR LOCAL DEPARTMENT STORE DOESN'T WANT YOU TO KNOW

WHAT YOUR LOCAL DEPARTMENT STORE DOESN'T WANT YOU TO KNOW

BASHEERAH SIMON

Inquiries and Book Orders should be addressed to:

Leavitt Peak Press
Email: info@leavittpeakpress.com Phone: 1-888-549-0988

ISBN: 979-8-90528-037-5 (sc)
ISBN: 979-8-90528-038-2 (ebook)

Rev 06/24/2026

DEDICATION

This book is dedicated to devoted shoppers and to all present and former associates. To those whose money comes easily, without a second thought, and to those who work hard for every dollar they earn. Yet when it comes to shopping, everyone wants to feel they can afford the merchandise of their choice.

In these pages, we will discuss things that may appear one way but are not always what they seem.

CONTENTS

INTRODUCTION

Every day, millions of consumers enter department stores believing they are purchasing brand-new, high-quality merchandise at unbeatable prices. Behind the polished displays, endless promotions, and attractive sales, however, exists another side of retail culture rarely discussed openly.

This book explores the hidden realities of department store shopping, consumer behavior, retail policies, employee experiences, and the psychology behind modern shopping habits. Through observations and firsthand retail experiences, the author reveals a perspective many shoppers never consider.

The Psychology of Shopping

Shopping has become a way of life for many people. Some shop because they need something important, while others shop because it makes them feel good. There are people who shop when they are happy, people who shop when they are depressed, and people who shop simply because they are bored and want something to do. No matter the reason, shopping has become deeply connected to emotions, habits, and personal desires.

For many customers, entering a department store creates a feeling of excitement. Bright lights, beautiful displays, music playing throughout the store, signs announcing sales everywhere, and racks filled with merchandise all work together to create an experience that attracts people in. Some customers walk through the doors with a shopping list, while others enter with no plans at all and still leave carrying bags full of merchandise.

Department stores understand human behavior very well. They know how to attract customers and how to encourage them to spend more money than they originally intended. Stores place sale signs in large bold letters, decorate entrances with attractive displays, and position popular merchandise in areas where customers are forced to walk past other tempting items. Many people believe they are simply shopping, but often they are responding emotionally to carefully planned marketing strategies.

One of the biggest attractions in retail is the word "sale." The moment customers hear that their favorite department store is having a sale, excitement begins immediately. Friends call each other, advertisements are checked, and plans are made to arrive early before the best items disappear. People become convinced they are saving money, even while spending more than they originally planned.

Sales have a powerful effect on the mind. A customer may enter a store intending to purchase one item and leave with five simply because the merchandise appeared to be discounted. Stores understand this psychology very well. They know customers are more likely to buy something when they believe they are getting a bargain.

Coupons also play a major role in shopping behavior. Many department stores send discount cards and coupons through the mail every month. Customers wait for these coupons and often refuse to shop without them. Some shoppers become upset if a coupon expires, even by a single day, and will argue with associates or managers to honor the discount anyway. In many cases, the store eventually gives in because they do not want to lose the customer's business.

Shopping is also a social activity. Some people enjoy spending an entire day at the mall with friends or family members. They stop for coffee, browse different departments, try on clothes, compare prices, and discuss what they might buy next. Sometimes people purchase things they never intended to buy simply because someone else encouraged them.

The mall itself creates a certain atmosphere. Customers move from store to store surrounded by sales signs, perfumes, clothing displays, food courts, music, and crowds of people carrying shopping bags. The environment creates excitement and encourages spending. Some shoppers feel proud walking through the mall with expensive store bags in their hands because it creates a feeling of status and importance.

For others, shopping becomes emotional comfort. There are people who shop after having a bad day because purchasing something makes them temporarily feel better. Some people use shopping to escape stress, loneliness, or disappointment. Even though the feeling may not last long, the excitement of buying something new gives them a temporary emotional lift.

Credit cards have also changed the psychology of shopping. Years ago, customers were limited by the cash they carried. Today, people can continue purchasing even when they do not actually have the money available at the moment. Department stores encourage this behavior by constantly promoting store credit cards with promises of discounts, rewards, and special privileges. Many customers open credit accounts just to receive an immediate discount on a purchase.

Stores carefully study spending habits and customer behavior. They know which departments attract the most attention, what products customers buy impulsively, and what displays encourage people to spend more time browsing. Every part of the shopping experience is designed to increase sales.

There is nothing wrong with shopping or enjoying nice things. Most people work hard for their money and deserve to buy things they enjoy. However, many customers never stop to think about how much influence department stores have over their decisions and emotions.

Retail stores understand the psychology of shopping better than most people realize.

That is what makes shopping such a powerful experience. It is not only about buying merchandise. It is about emotion, desire, appearance, excitement, and sometimes even escape. Behind every sale sign and every beautiful display is a business strategy designed to encourage customers to spend.

And most of the time, it works.

The Power of Sales and Discounts

Nothing captures the attention of shoppers faster than the word "sale." The moment customers hear that a department store is having a special event, excitement begins immediately. Advertisements appear everywhere, phones start ringing, and people begin making plans to visit the store before the best merchandise disappears. Sales create urgency, competition, and emotion all at the same time.

Department stores understand this very well. Sales are not simply random discounts. They are carefully planned events designed to increase traffic, encourage impulse buying, and create excitement among customers. Many shoppers walk into a store believing they are saving money, while in reality they often spend far more than they originally intended.

There was a time when department stores held what were called "Dollar Day Sales." Customers rushed into stores believing they were getting unbelievable bargains because everything appeared to cost only one dollar. What many customers did not realize was that some items that normally sold for less than a dollar were raised to one dollar for the event. Merchandise priced at fifty cents, seventy-nine cents, or eighty-nine cents suddenly became part of the "Dollar Sale." Even so, customers continued buying because the idea of getting a bargain was more powerful than the actual savings.

Retail stores have always relied on psychology to increase sales. The techniques may have changed over the years, but the goal remains the same — get customers excited enough to spend money. Long ago, stores used large newspaper advertisements and window displays to attract shoppers. Today, stores use emails, text alerts, social media, online promotions, and loyalty programs to create the same excitement.

Coupons are another powerful tool used by department stores. Many customers wait for coupons before shopping because they believe they are receiving exclusive savings. Some shoppers refuse to purchase anything unless they have a discount card in hand. Others become angry if a coupon has expired, even by one day, and demand that the store honor it anyway.

Associates often find themselves caught in uncomfortable situations because of these discount policies. Employees are trained to follow store rules, but when customers complain loudly enough, managers sometimes ignore the policies completely just to satisfy the customer. This can leave the associate looking embarrassed or powerless in front of everyone.

Many customers also believe they are winning when they use discounts, rewards cards, and coupons together. Stores encourage this thinking because customers who believe they are saving money usually spend more freely. A shopper may purchase several unnecessary items simply because they feel the discount is too good to pass up.

Department stores are designed to make customers stay longer and spend more money. Sale racks are often placed near entrances to immediately attract attention. Clearance signs create urgency, making customers feel they must buy quickly before someone else does. Bright signs saying "Limited Time Only" or "Final Markdown" create pressure even when the merchandise may remain available for weeks.

Some customers become extremely emotional during large sales events. They argue over merchandise, demand additional discounts, and compete with other shoppers for popular items. During holiday sales and clearance events, stores can become chaotic. Associates are expected to remain calm and polite no matter how demanding or aggressive customers become.

For many people, shopping during a sale feels exciting and rewarding. Customers leave the store carrying multiple bags, convinced they made smart financial decisions because they purchased items at reduced prices. However, stores profit greatly from these events because increased volume often brings in far more revenue than regular shopping days.

Sales also create a sense of status for some shoppers. Certain customers take pride in knowing how to combine discounts, coupons, store cards, and rewards programs to maximize savings. Others become loyal to specific department stores because they enjoy feeling like preferred customers.

Behind every successful sale is careful planning. Stores study customer habits, shopping patterns, and spending behavior in great detail. They know what colors attract attention, which departments bring in the most traffic, and how pricing influences customer decisions. Even the arrangement of merchandise is designed to encourage impulse purchases.

Many shoppers never stop to think about how much strategy goes into creating a sale. They simply see excitement, discounts, and opportunities to buy something they want. What customers often do not realize is that the store has already studied their behavior long before they walked through the doors.

Sales are powerful because they appeal to emotion. They create excitement, urgency, satisfaction, and sometimes even competition. Customers may believe they are fully in control of their spending decisions, but department stores understand exactly how to encourage people to buy more.

That is the true power behind sales and discounts. They do far more than reduce prices. They influence behavior, shape spending habits, and keep customers returning again and again.

Department Store Credit Cards

One of the biggest tools department stores use to keep customers spending is the store credit card. Many customers do not realize how important these credit cards are to retail businesses. To the customer, it may seem like a simple way to save a few dollars, but to the store it is a powerful business strategy designed to create loyalty and increase spending.

Almost every department store today pushes customers to apply for a store credit card. The moment customers approach the register, associates are often required to ask if they would like to open an account. Customers are promised immediate discounts, bonus rewards, special coupons, and exclusive shopping privileges if they apply right away.

For many shoppers, the temptation is difficult to resist. A customer may arrive planning to spend fifty dollars, but when offered twenty percent off for opening a credit account, they suddenly begin shopping for more items to "take advantage" of the discount. What appears to be savings often leads to more spending.

Many associates are placed under tremendous pressure to get customers to apply for these cards. In some stores, employee performance is measured heavily by how many credit applications they produce during the week. Associates who fail to meet expectations may receive poor evaluations, fewer work hours, or no raises at all.

This creates stress throughout the store. Employees begin focusing less on helping customers and more on convincing them to open accounts. Some associates become extremely aggressive with sales tactics because their jobs may depend on it. Others feel uncomfortable pressuring customers but fear management consequences if they do not meet quotas.

There are employees who will go above and beyond to secure applications. Some promise additional discounts or make customers feel guilty for refusing. Associates may repeatedly ask customers throughout the transaction even after the customer has already said no. Many shoppers become irritated by the constant pressure, while others eventually give in simply to avoid further conversation.

Customers with store credit cards are often treated differently from regular shoppers. Department stores value these customers because they usually spend more money and return more frequently. Some customers even use their store status as leverage when speaking with management or associates.

It is not uncommon for certain shoppers to say things such as, "I spend a lot of money in this store," or "I have one of your top credit accounts." Some customers believe this gives them special authority, and sometimes management reinforces that belief by giving in to complaints, exceptions, or return requests simply to avoid losing their business.

The store's main goal is to keep customers returning again and again. Credit cards help accomplish this because customers feel connected to the store through rewards programs, discounts, and monthly offers. Coupons arrive regularly in the mail encouraging customers to return for another sale or promotion.

Many customers do not fully realize how quickly store credit debt can grow. A person may make small purchases over time believing they are manageable, only to discover later that interest charges and continued spending have created a large balance. Department stores profit greatly from customers who continue carrying balances month after month.

For some shoppers, credit creates the illusion of affordability. A customer may purchase expensive clothing, furniture, or household items they normally could not pay for with cash simply because the credit card allows delayed payments. The excitement of shopping often overshadows the reality of future bills.

Stores understand the emotional connection customers have with shopping. They know many people enjoy feeling important, rewarded, and valued. Exclusive cardholder events, special discounts, and reward programs are all designed to strengthen that emotional attachment.

Behind the scenes, associates are also affected by this system. Employees are constantly reminded about credit goals, customer sign- ups, and store performance. In some environments, workers feel more like sales machines than actual human beings. They may provide excellent customer service all day long, but if they fail to produce enough credit applications, management may still consider them unsuccessful.

This pressure creates frustration among many retail employees. Associates work hard helping customers, cleaning departments, organizing merchandise, and handling difficult situations, yet much of their value becomes measured by numbers rather than effort or professionalism.

Department store credit cards have become deeply connected to modern retail culture. They influence how customers shop, how employees are evaluated, and how stores generate profit. To many shoppers, the card may appear harmless or convenient. To the store, however, it represents customer loyalty, increased spending, and long-term business.

That is why department stores push credit cards so heavily. They are not simply offering customers another way to pay. They are creating a system designed to keep people shopping, returning, and spending for years to come.

Customer Behavior and Store Culture

Every department store attracts all kinds of people. Customers come from different backgrounds, income levels, cultures, and lifestyles, yet once they enter the store, many of their shopping habits begin to look surprisingly similar. No matter who they are outside the store, the excitement of shopping often places everyone into the same environment with the same goal — finding something they want.

Some customers shop calmly and respectfully, while others enter the store already demanding attention. There are customers who enjoy browsing quietly, and there are those who immediately expect special treatment the moment they walk through the doors. Retail associates quickly learn how differently people behave while shopping.

There are customers who believe money gives them authority over everyone in the store. Some demand immediate assistance, special discounts, or exceptions to store policies simply because they spend large amounts of money there. Others constantly remind associates about their store credit status, reward memberships, or relationships with management.

Then there are the customers who want to appear important. These are often the shoppers who loudly ask for managers, insist on special treatment, or become offended when things do not go exactly their way. Some customers create scenes over expired coupons, denied discounts, or merchandise that is no longer available.

Associates are expected to remain polite no matter how difficult the situation becomes. Even when customers speak disrespectfully or behave aggressively, employees are usually instructed to stay calm and avoid conflict. In many cases, management sides with the customer simply to protect business and avoid complaints.

This creates an uncomfortable environment for many retail workers. Employees may follow store policies correctly, only to have managers reverse decisions moments later in front of customers. When this happens repeatedly, associates begin feeling unsupported and embarrassed.

Some shoppers truly believe in the saying, "The customer is always right." While good customer service is important, there are situations where customers misuse that belief to pressure employees into breaking rules or making exceptions. Associates often feel powerless because they know management may eventually give the customer whatever they want.

Shopping also affects how people see themselves socially. Some customers feel proud shopping in expensive stores because it creates a feeling of status or importance. Others may feel uncomfortable entering stores they consider too upscale or expensive. Clothing, appearance, and surroundings can influence confidence while shopping.

There are also customers who carefully observe others while they shop. People notice what brands others carry, how they dress, and how much they spend. Shopping environments often become places where people silently compare themselves to others.

Interestingly, some wealthy or well-known individuals behave far more respectfully than customers trying hardest to appear important. There are shoppers who quietly purchase expensive merchandise without arguments, coupons, or complaints. They simply buy what they want and leave without drawing attention to themselves.

On the other hand, some customers become extremely emotional over small discounts or minor inconveniences. Associates witness arguments over sale prices, expired coupons, and return policies almost every day. During major sales, customer behavior can become especially intense as people compete for merchandise and bargains.

Department stores themselves help shape this behavior. The environment is designed to encourage spending, excitement, and emotional reactions. Bright displays, music, sales signs, and crowded shopping events all contribute to the atmosphere customers experience.

Store culture also affects employees. Associates are expected to smile constantly, remain friendly under pressure, and satisfy customers no matter how stressful conditions become. Workers must balance store policies, customer expectations, management pressure, and sales goals all at once.

Many employees eventually begin to feel less like people and more like part of the store machinery. They are expected to tolerate disrespect, maintain perfect attitudes, and continue performing under difficult conditions because customer satisfaction is treated as the highest priority.

Despite all of this, retail workers continue showing up every day helping customers, organizing merchandise, cleaning departments, and trying to maintain order in busy environments. Most customers never fully see the pressure associates face behind the scenes.

Department stores are more than places to buy merchandise. They are environments where personalities, emotions, social behavior, and business pressures all collide together. Customers may see only the polished appearance of the store, but behind the displays and sales signs is a complicated culture driven by money, expectations, and human behavior.

That culture affects everyone inside the store

— the customers spending money, the managers protecting business, and especially the associates trying to survive another long day on the sales floor.

Behind the Dressing Room Curtain

Most customers walk into a department store believing the merchandise surrounding them is completely fresh, untouched, and brand new. Clothes are neatly arranged, folded carefully on tables, and displayed beautifully under bright lights. Everything appears clean, organized, and perfect from the outside. What many customers never think about is what happens behind the dressing room curtain.

The dressing room is one of the busiest and most chaotic areas in many department stores. Throughout the day, customers enter carrying armfuls of clothing to try on piece after piece searching for the perfect size, color, or style. Some customers treat the fitting rooms respectfully, but many do not.

Associates often watch customers walk into dressing rooms carrying ten or fifteen items at a time. Some stores limit the number of pieces customers may take inside, while others allow as many as the customer wants. After trying everything on, many shoppers simply leave unwanted clothing piled on benches, hanging halfway off hangers, thrown across chairs, or crumpled on the floor.

Employees then spend hours cleaning those rooms, rehanging clothes, refolding merchandise, organizing racks, and returning everything back to the sales floor so the next customer sees a neat and attractive display. This process repeats itself all day long.

What customers often fail to realize is that many of the clothes hanging on department store racks have already been tried on multiple times before being purchased. Some garments may have passed through dozens of fitting rooms, touched countless hands, and been dropped on floors repeatedly before someone finally buys them.

There are also customers who walk around the store wearing clothing they are still deciding whether to purchase. They may continue shopping, trying on other items, or carrying the clothes throughout the store before eventually returning them to the fitting room. Sometimes the clothing is left wrinkled, stained with makeup, or carrying strong odors from perfume, smoke, or body odor.

Associates regularly discover clothing with deodorant marks, makeup stains, food spots, wrinkles, and other signs of wear. Some customers return merchandise after wearing it to events, dinners, or social gatherings and claim the items simply "didn't fit." In certain situations, returned merchandise may accidentally make its way back onto the sales floor if the condition is overlooked.

There have also been instances where customers return clothing carrying cigarette smoke, pet hair, or heavy perfume scents. Other garments are found turned completely inside out, stretched, or damaged from repeated handling. Yet many shoppers still believe the merchandise hanging neatly on display racks has never been touched before.

The dressing rooms themselves can become extremely unpleasant. Associates often describe entering fitting rooms filled with piles of clothing stacked high on benches and floors. Zippers may be broken, hangers bent, and merchandise scattered everywhere. Employees are responsible for restoring order no matter how messy conditions become.

Some situations become far worse than simple clutter. Retail workers have shared stories of dressing rooms being misused in shocking ways, including customers leaving behind food, trash, bodily waste, or heavily soiled merchandise. When situations like this occur, dressing rooms sometimes must be temporarily closed so housekeeping can disinfect and clean the area.

Years ago, many stores assigned attendants specifically to monitor dressing rooms and discourage theft or inappropriate behavior. Today, stores often operate with fewer employees while expecting associates to manage multiple responsibilities at once. As a result, dressing rooms may go unattended for long periods during busy shopping hours.

The fitting room is also one of the main areas where theft occurs. Some customers enter carrying large bags from other stores, making it easier to hide unpaid merchandise. Associates sometimes discover security tags removed and hidden in corners or underneath piles of clothes. Others find empty hangers or tags left behind after merchandise disappears.

Professional shoplifters understand store policies and employee limitations very well. Some customers even wear stolen merchandise out of the store while leaving behind older clothing inside the fitting room. Others later attempt to return stolen items for store credit or refunds without receipts.

Despite all of this, department stores continue presenting an image of cleanliness, luxury, and perfection. Beautiful displays and carefully arranged racks create the appearance that everything inside the store is untouched and flawless. Most customers never stop to think about what those clothes may have experienced before arriving in their shopping bags.

Interestingly, many people criticize thrift stores for selling used clothing while proudly purchasing department store merchandise that has already been handled, tried on, worn temporarily, returned, and repeatedly placed back onto the sales floor. The difference is often more about perception than reality.

This hidden side of retail is something many department stores prefer customers not think about too deeply. Shoppers see polished displays and attractive packaging, but employees working behind the scenes witness the daily reality that most customers never imagine.

Behind the dressing room curtain lies a completely different version of the department store experience — one far less glamorous than the image presented on the sales floor.

Department Stores vs. Thrift Stores

Many people look at department stores and thrift stores as completely different worlds. One is often viewed as clean, modern, fashionable, and respectable, while the other is sometimes unfairly judged as old, used, or lower in status. However, when you take a closer look at both environments, the differences are not always as large as people imagine.

At one time or another, most people have visited a thrift store. Some go searching for bargains, others look for rare finds, furniture, household items, or clothing at affordable prices. There are shoppers who proudly shop at thrift stores, and there are others who would never admit they shop there at all.

Walking into a thrift store can feel surprisingly similar to entering a department store. Customers browse through racks of clothing, look at shoes, handbags, furniture, dishes, decorations, and household merchandise. There are shelves filled with glassware, lamps, picture frames, cookware, and electronics. Items are arranged by sections just like they are in larger retail stores.

The biggest difference is perception.

In a department store, customers believe they are purchasing something brand new. In a thrift store, customers already understand the merchandise has been previously owned. Because of that expectation, people mentally accept flaws, wear, and imperfections before they even begin shopping.

What many shoppers fail to realize is that department store merchandise often goes through far more handling than customers think. Clothes are tried on repeatedly, dropped on fitting room floors, returned after being worn, handled by countless customers, and placed back onto racks day after day. Some items may sit on the sales floor for months being touched constantly before finally being sold.

In a thrift store, customers already know the clothing has been used before. Ironically, many thrift stores clean, organize, steam, or inspect merchandise carefully before placing it out for sale. Yet some shoppers still view department store merchandise as "cleaner" simply because it hangs inside a more polished environment.

Department stores rely heavily on presentation. Bright lighting, clean floors, soft music, organized displays, and attractive decorations create the appearance of luxury and perfection. Customers often associate beautiful presentation with higher quality and cleanliness.

Thrift stores usually focus less on appearance and more on affordability and practicality. The décor may be simpler, racks may feel more crowded, and the environment may not look as polished. Because of this, many people judge the merchandise differently even when the reality may not be very different at all.

Shopping habits also change depending on the environment. In department stores, customers may feel pressure to look fashionable, important, or financially comfortable. Some shoppers become concerned with image and status while walking through expensive stores carrying branded shopping bags.

At thrift stores, the atmosphere is often more relaxed. Customers usually focus more on finding value than impressing anyone else. People search carefully through racks hoping to discover hidden treasures, unique items, or excellent bargains.

Interestingly, some of the same behaviors seen in department stores also appear in thrift stores. Customers still argue over prices, compete for merchandise, and search aggressively for the best deals. The excitement of finding something valuable at a low price exists in both environments.

There are also people who believe shopping at certain stores reflects social status. Some customers proudly avoid thrift stores because they associate them with poverty or struggle, while others shop there confidently without embarrassment. In reality, people from many different financial backgrounds visit thrift stores for many different reasons.

Department stores and thrift stores both depend on customer psychology. One sells the image of luxury, exclusivity, and "newness." The other sells affordability, practicality, and opportunity. Both environments encourage emotional spending in different ways.

Furniture sections offer another interesting comparison. In department stores, customers sit on couches, lie on beds, test chairs, and handle merchandise throughout the day. Display furniture may remain on the floor being touched constantly by hundreds of people. Yet customers still consider it completely new because it comes from a department store setting.

Meanwhile, thrift store furniture is openly acknowledged as previously owned, even though some pieces may have received less handling overall than heavily displayed department store items. Again, perception shapes the customer's thinking more than reality itself.

The same idea applies to clothing. Customers in department stores may try on large piles of garments, leave makeup stains, wrinkles, perfume odors, or deodorant marks, and return items after wearing them briefly. Yet many shoppers continue believing these clothes are untouched simply because they are displayed in a beautiful environment.

This comparison is not meant to criticize department stores or praise thrift stores unfairly. It is simply meant to make customers think differently about what they are purchasing and how retail presentation influences perception.

At the end of the day, both types of stores are businesses trying to attract customers and make sales. One uses polished presentation and branding to create value. The other uses affordability and practicality.

But when it comes to human behavior, customer habits, and the reality of merchandise handling, the two worlds may not be as different as many people believe.

The Reality of Retail Employees

Most customers see only one side of a department store. They see clean displays, smiling associates, sale signs, and organized merchandise. What they often do not see is the pressure, stress, and emotional exhaustion many retail employees experience behind the scenes every single day.

Working in retail is far more demanding than many people realize. Associates are expected to remain pleasant no matter what situation they face. They must greet customers warmly, answer endless questions, organize merchandise, clean departments, recover fitting rooms, process returns, handle complaints, and still meet sales expectations all at the same time.

Many stores constantly remind employees that customer satisfaction comes first. While good customer service is important, some retail environments take this idea so far that associates begin feeling like their own dignity matters less than keeping customers happy.

There are employees who work extremely hard yet still feel unappreciated. Associates may follow company policies exactly as they were trained, only to have managers reverse decisions in front of customers moments later.

This leaves workers feeling embarrassed and unsupported.

One of the biggest pressures placed on retail employees involves store credit cards and sales goals. In many department stores, associates are judged heavily by numbers — how many credit applications they open, how many rewards programs they promote, or how many additional items they convince customers to buy.

Employees who fail to meet these expectations may receive poor evaluations, reduced hours, or missed raises. Some workers become so worried about performance that they constantly pressure customers to apply for store credit cards even when customers clearly are not interested.

This pressure affects the entire work environment. Instead of focusing completely on customer service, employees often feel forced to think constantly about quotas and numbers. Some workers begin competing against one another for sales and credit applications because management rewards those with the highest performance numbers.

Associates also deal with difficult customer behavior on a regular basis. There are customers who speak disrespectfully, demand special treatment, or become angry over small inconveniences. Some customers act as though employees are personal servants rather than human beings doing a job.

Retail workers are often expected to tolerate behavior they would never accept outside the workplace. Customers may raise their voices, insult employees, make unreasonable demands, or threaten to take their business elsewhere if they do not get what they want. In many situations, management sides with the customer simply to avoid complaints or lost sales.

This creates frustration and emotional exhaustion among employees. Workers begin feeling powerless because they know defending themselves may put their jobs at risk. Some associates become afraid to speak honestly at all because one customer complaint could lead to disciplinary action.

Many employees remain in these situations because they need steady income and cannot afford to lose their jobs. Retail work may appear simple from the outside, but for many associates it involves long hours standing on hard floors, dealing with constant pressure, and managing stressful customer interactions throughout the day.

Pay is another major issue in retail environments. Many associates work extremely hard while earning low wages with limited opportunities for advancement. Some employees feel stores expect complete loyalty and dedication while offering very little financial reward in return.

Workers often observe unfair behavior within the system itself. Some employees may bend rules to increase sales numbers or gain management approval. Others become discouraged when they see favoritism or inconsistent treatment between workers.

Despite these challenges, many retail employees continue doing their jobs professionally every day. Associates help customers find merchandise, maintain store appearance, clean departments, process complicated transactions, and handle stressful situations with patience that often goes unnoticed.

Customers rarely see the amount of work happening behind the scenes before the store opens or after it closes. Employees spend hours reorganizing racks, cleaning dressing rooms, returning misplaced merchandise, changing displays, and preparing the store for another day of business.

Retail associates also witness human behavior at its best and worst. Some customers are kind, patient, and appreciative. Others create chaos, disrespect workers, or treat employees as though they are invisible. Over time, these experiences shape how many workers feel about the retail industry itself.

The reality is that department stores could not function without the associates working on the sales floor every day. Employees are the ones helping customers, maintaining order, and carrying the pressure of keeping the business running smoothly.

Yet many workers feel they are treated as replaceable rather than valuable.

Behind the polished appearance of every department store are employees carrying stress, frustration, exhaustion, and pressure that most customers never fully recognize. The smiling associate greeting customers at the register may be dealing with impossible sales goals, management pressure, rude customers, and physical exhaustion all at once.

That is the hidden reality many people never think about when they walk into a department store.

The Men's Department: A Different Retail Experience

When people think about department store shopping, most of the stories and experiences shared by employees tend to come from women's departments. Conversations about fitting rooms, overflowing racks, fashion trends, and customer interactions often focus on women's apparel because it typically receives more attention and generates higher traffic. As a result, very little is written or discussed about the men's department.

Among retail associates, the men's department is often considered one of the more manageable areas of the store. Many employees, including female associates, enjoy working there because the environment is usually calmer and less hectic than other departments. While every store is different, men's departments often experience fewer fitting room issues, less merchandise left behind, and fewer daily recovery challenges compared to areas with heavier customer traffic.

This does not mean the men's department is without responsibility. Associates still assist customers with sizing, product selection, and merchandise presentation. They help customers coordinate dress shirts, ties, belts, shoes, sports coats, and business attire. During special occasions such as weddings, graduations, job interviews, and formal events, associates often spend significant time helping customers build complete outfits that fit both their style and budget.

One unique aspect of the men's department involves fitting room assistance. While female associates can assist with most merchandise throughout the department, certain situations involving suit fittings or more personal fitting room requests may require male associates to provide direct assistance. This creates a slightly different dynamic than what is commonly seen in women's departments.

Another noticeable difference is customer behavior. Many men tend to approach shopping with a specific purpose in mind. They often enter the store looking for a particular item, make their selection, and complete their purchase relatively quickly. While there are certainly exceptions, the shopping experience in men's departments is frequently more straightforward and less emotionally driven than in other retail areas.

Because of these differences, the men's department rarely generates the dramatic stories that employees often share from other sections of the store. There are fewer disputes over fitting rooms, fewer abandoned piles of merchandise, and generally fewer situations that become memorable for the wrong reasons.

Perhaps that is why so little is written about the men's department. It quietly operates as one of the more predictable areas of the store. While it may not produce the same volume of stories as other departments, it remains an important part of the retail experience, serving customers who value convenience, practicality, and efficiency in their shopping journey.

Final Thoughts: What Stores Don't Want You to Notice

Department stores are designed to create a certain experience. The lighting is carefully arranged, the merchandise is organized attractively, music plays throughout the building, and displays are created to make customers feel comfortable, excited, and ready to spend money. Everything customers see is part of a larger system designed to encourage shopping.

Most people walk into stores thinking only about what they want to buy. Very few stop to think about what happens behind the scenes — the pressure on employees, the condition of returned merchandise, the emotional tactics used during sales, or the way customer behavior changes inside these environments.

This book was never written to stop people from shopping. Shopping is part of everyday life. People work hard for their money and deserve to enjoy buying things for themselves and their families. The purpose of this book is simply to encourage awareness.

Customers often see only the polished side of retail. They see beautiful displays and smiling associates, but they rarely see the stress employees experience daily. They do not always realize how much pressure workers face to satisfy customers, open credit accounts, meet sales goals, and remain calm under difficult conditions.

Many shoppers also never think about the reality behind the merchandise itself. Clothing may have been tried on countless times, returned after being worn, dropped on dressing room floors, or handled by dozens of people before finally being purchased. Yet department stores continue presenting everything as fresh and untouched.

The truth is that retail is built heavily on perception. Stores sell more than merchandise — they sell image, emotion, status, excitement, and desire. Customers are encouraged to feel successful, fashionable, important, or rewarded through shopping experiences carefully created by the retail industry.

Sales and discounts create urgency. Credit cards create spending freedom. Store rewards create loyalty. Beautiful displays create emotional attraction. All of these things work together to keep customers returning again and again.

At the same time, employees often carry the burden of maintaining this system. Associates stand for long hours, deal with difficult situations, clean up after customers, reorganize departments repeatedly, and work under constant pressure to protect the store's image.

There are good customers and difficult customers. There are good managers and difficult managers. There are honest employees and dishonest ones. Retail stores bring together every type of personality and behavior imaginable under one roof every single day.

What makes retail interesting is not just the merchandise being sold. It is the human behavior that unfolds inside the store — the emotions, attitudes, frustrations, desires, and social interactions happening constantly between customers and employees.

Some people shop for necessity. Others shop for comfort, entertainment, or emotional escape. Some customers seek bargains while others seek status. Some workers genuinely enjoy helping people, while others remain in retail simply because they need employment and stability.

No matter the reason, department stores continue playing a major role in everyday life. Millions of people walk through their doors each year without fully realizing how much psychology, pressure, strategy, and human emotion operate behind the scenes.

The retail world is far more complicated than most customers imagine.

This book is simply an attempt to pull back the curtain for a moment and allow readers to see another side of that world — the side employees witness every day but customers rarely notice.

Perhaps after reading this book, shoppers may think differently the next time they enter a department store. Maybe they will become more aware of how sales influence spending habits, how employees are treated, or how much work goes into maintaining the appearance of perfection.

And perhaps they may even look at the people working behind the counters with a little more understanding and respect.

Because behind every clean display, every organized rack, every fitting room, and every smiling associate is a reality most department stores never openly discuss.

www.ingramcontent.com/pod-product-compliance
Lightning Source LLC
LaVergne TN
LVHW050923210926
848482LV00012B/523
* 9 7 9 8 9 0 5 2 8 0 3 7 5 *